DATE DUE

THE F   CTUAL

THE FEELING IS ACTUAL

Paolo Javier

Marsh Hawk Press
East Rockaway, New York 2011

FIRST EDITION

Marsh Hawk Press books are published by Poetry Mailing List, Inc., a not-for-profit corporation under section 501 (c) 3 United States Internal Revenue Code.

Book and cover design: Tim Peterson (Trace)
Thanks Garamond, Clarendon, Matrix and Lemonade
Cover font is "Goudy Grunge," an original typeface by the designer

Cover Photo: Emmy Catedral
Illustrations: Alex Tarampi
Author Photo: 劉恬恬

ISBN-13: 978-0-9846353-3-7 (pbk.)
ISBN-10: 0-9846353-3-5 (pbk.)

 **Marsh Hawk Press**
P.O. Box 206, East Rockaway, N.Y. 11518-0206
www.marshhawkpress.org

Contents

Ladies and Gentlemen—Mr. Bill Murray!

This Pepperoni   8

You Were Delivering a Single   9

Ladies and Gentlemen—Mr. Bill Murray!   15

F Y E O

Pinoy Signs   27

Funny Love   32

Field Report   35

from LMFAO   36

L M F A O   37

Wolfgang Amadeus Bigfoot   73

Heart as Arena

Batman That One   92

gh_t   97

Heart as Arena   107

Monty & Turtle   119

Feeling Its Actual   135

Ladies and Gentlemen—Mr. Bill Murray!

This Pepperoni

is a one-
of-a-
kind

you'd love it too
if you
were
pepperoni-inclined

it's got big, big flavor!
would you do me a big-big favor?

come share this lonely
pepperoni
          with me?

You Were Delivering a Single

you were about to get into the rhythm, &
      your weight was on your back foot
when you demonstrated that beauty knew no bounds

you were clearly the 1
you were clearly playing better than anyone
you were the reigning Open champion
      of the heart's floodlit court

you were the value
you were #1 among the constellations,
      & Venus #2

I always felt that you were beautiful in the classical sense
        of the Ur
you were a young woman who's always faced the challenges of life with cerebral poesy
you were a sweet 14 year old
you were 2
you were 24
you were a born survivor
you were otherwise known online as Saint Clara

once, during our first month together, on the last leg of an unplanned trip into the Valley
you drove me to a beautiful rented home in Rocky Point
situated at a short distance from Milan
located in Manzanillo
one of Chile's oldest cities next to
one of Chile's oldest towns
it was a city of old world charm then
it was a city with a population of just over a hundred
& you were their memory resident

you were a flame
you were a pleasant sea
you were the word for mermaid in the Philippines
you were a pair of mango-juice stained fingertips
you were a birthday backrub & a lingering kiss
you were chocolate

then one day you died in my arms in a dream
where I got usurped by a powerful player
    with a killer serve
who was always much more gregarious
who was sure to impress anyone upon arrival

now this powerful player
is neither 24 years old nor attends Juban Junior High School in Tokyo
is not as good as Venus once could have been
is not a black smoke British shorthair born May 18
is not your fabulous imported shire mare
is way behind in any of those categories compared to the players with which he will
    surely be judged in time

I was determined to drive out this interloper
    & his household of man-servants

you were no longer a welcome guest in my house

you were hurt, but
you were unbeaten, &
because of that

you're probably off right now apartment-hunting in the margins of Brooklyn
        to be near him

& you will serve
& you will volley
& you will deliver it to me
      blow-by-blow

& these last three are the only things about you
I would ever truly want anyone here to know

Ladies and Gentlemen—Mr. Bill Murray!

Do we call it a love story? Usually
love stories are sort of sappy.
I think of people dying in the end.

      You know I've always wanted
to shoot our movie. I always felt I could perform
well in it, given the kind of person that I am—
a man who's neither sentimental nor a shmaltz,
but loves romance. I think it's the greatest thing
in the world.

For years, I've thought, I really wish I could
do that—be part of a reel of film in someone's life
that makes you laugh & cry with each viewing. I see
others project their silvery dreams onto the screen,
but I always think it's sort of like how one perceives
one's self in one's underwear—making oneself into some
sort of terribly hot person. But isn't it great to just fall
in love?

I really thought I could do this, I've thought
about it for a long time, because every good romance
has comedy in it. Ask anyone: he's got to be able to make
you laugh. You need that. We may never agree on Arnold
taking office, but we can agree on what's funny. You make me
laugh, & we are the same, we're not alone anymore, really.

& it shouldn't be painful, it shouldn't end in death
or disease; it's possible to be a romantic without being either
dead or sad or unfaithful. There is a way to live such a life
without hurting a single person.

Because a man gets in a situation
where he either apologizes for his life,
or uses it to challenge what he wants
from the situation he finds himself in.

Because I've been there, & I'm familiar
with that scene where your character's on the horns
of a major dilemma, & the automatic thing is to
decide that this scene is more important than
any of the previous:

"I would rather be with you here
than with anyone else in the world."

I'm really stoked by that
because it really is the opposite of what
you usually hear.

Usually you hear how his wife's a bitch,
or that his kids are a fucking nightmare, or how
they hate his guts. You know—people lying
to get through an uncomfortable moment.

Not to make it sound melodramatic,
but when you're in that scene & you don't
take the easy way out, you always feel
so much better & so much more whole.
In the communal darkness of the cinema,
you listen to the person sitting next to you
think out loud about your performance:

"Holy shit, I just didn't hear
the same old crap from that guy."

Or like that moment when you ask a friend
to respond to a reading given by your favorite poet, &
you take it as a given that her ensuing silence is
the result of her lack of interest in it, rather than
her wonder over her exposure to poetry's radiation,
when all of a sudden she mentions:

"That is one nutty hospital."

Because I think when you're not feeling great
you want to make a grand gesture. I've been
a grand-gesture guy in the past. & in all likelihood,
I will continue to be one in the future. However,
I don't feel as grand gesture-ish as I once did.
Probably a good sign, don't you think?

It would have been a great night, an incredible night. But it also would have made the rest of our characters' lives unsatisfying. I think that my character probably knew this, but didn't understand it completely. In order to circumvent one thing from taking place, you do another thing that keeps it from happening: I'm going to show you my warts, or my tighty-whities with a huge rip in the center, so that in-between our final scenes together, neither one of us end up shooting too many close-ups.

Because you would have had to lead the rest of your life after,
& I could ruin your image of me now rather than do this other thing.

Because you're going to lead the rest of your life after,
& I could ruin the rest of your life now if you'll let me.

But I don't want that.

Oh my character was really in shape when he showed up.
He was really in shape. He was twenty pounds less than I will be
a month from now.

He was Nic Cage. No, he was Rosanna Arquette.
Actually, he was much lighter than that. But he was really quite fit,
lean, & hungry, really hungry to work hard. Let us go to another world,
let us conduct our scenes in another country where neither one of us speaks
the language. & I thought, well, shit, you know, I've been in that situation.
I know how valuable it is to erase your regular stuff & just work,
not take anything more than you need.

For once, I just wanted to play the romantic lead.
& this time, he came through. Right up until the credits,
my character comes through. He turns out to be a romantic guy
who can sing, who can write books, who can even play golf.

Before I go, let me lead you back to that scene
where my character walks onto the austere course
with Mt. Fuji looming in the distance. You know what?
He really crushes the ball. Two-ninety-five it was.
& I swear to you, his swagger, as he walks off the tee

is absolutely real.

FYEO

Production Note

Four sets of projections occur in sequence during the performance of FYEO:

1. Pinoy Signs

2. Funny Love

3. Field Report

4. from LMFAO (OMG!)

Pinoy Signs: Signs with unclear images are read out loud for audience recognition.

Funny Love: Allow for images to linger, with measured scrolling in-between.

from LMFAO: Slide projection beginning on page 22.

Projection 1   # Pinoy Signs

Nury Vittachi:

This week, we shall take a "reading tour" of one of the most spirited communities in Asia. The Philippines is full of word play. The local accent among many Filipinos, in which English words with F are spelled and pronounced with the sound of P and V is pronounced as B (because the Philippine alphabet has no letters F or V), is often used very cleverly, such as the sign in a flower shop in Dilliman called Petal Attraction.

Much of the word play in the Philippines is deliberate with retailers and various businesses favoring a play on names of Western establishments and celebrities (Americans, in particular; movie stars and entertainment personalities, especially)

For example, there is a bread shop in Manila called Anita Bakery, a 24-hour restaurant called Doris Day and Night, a garment shop called Elizabeth Tailoring, and a barbershop called Felix The Cut.

Reader Robert Harland also spotted a bakery named Bread Pitt, and a Makati fast-food place selling maruya (banana fritters) called Maruya Carey. Then, there is Christopher Plumbing; a boutique called The Way We Wear; a video rental shop called Leon King Video Rental; a restaurant in the Cainta district of Rizal called Caintacky Fried Chicken; a local burger restaurant called Mang Donald's; a doughnut shop called MacDonuts; a shop selling lumpia (egg roll) in Makati called Wrap and Roll; and two butcher shops called Meating Place and Meatropolis.

Smart travelers can decipher what may look like baffling signs to unaccustomed foreigners by simply sounding out the Taglish (the Philippine version of English words spelled and pronounced with a heavy Filipino accent), such as, at a restaurant menu in Cebu : "We hab sopdrink in can an in batol" [translation: We have soft drinks in can and in bottle]. Then, there is a sewing accessories shop called Bids And Pises [translation: Beads and Pieces —or— Bits and Pieces].

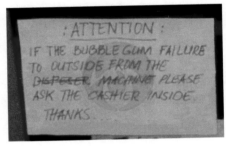

There are also many signs with either badly chosen or misspelled words, but they are usually so entertaining that it would be a mistake to "correct" them. A reader named Antonio 'Tonyboy' Ramon T. Ongsiako, (now there's a truly Filipino name), contributed the following interesting Philippine signs and advertisements: in a restaurant in Baguio City (the "summer capital" of the Philippines), "Wanted: Boy Waitress"; on a highway in Pampanga, "We Make Modern Antique Furniture"; on the window of a photography shop in Cabanatuan, "We Shoot You While You Wait"; and on the glass front of a cafe in Panay Avenue in Manila, "Wanted: Waiter, Cashier, Washier."

Some of the notices can even give a wrong impression, such as a shoe store in Pangasinan which has a sign saying: "We Sell Imported Robber Shoes" (these could be the sneakiest sneakers); and a rental property sign in Jaro, Iloilo reads: "House For Rent, Fully Furnaced" (it must really be hot inside)!

Occasionally, one could come across signs that are truly unique, if not altogether odd. Reader Gunilla Edlund submitted a sign that she saw at the ticket booth in the ferry pier in Davao City in southern Philippines, which announced: "Adults: 1 peso; Child: 50 centavos; Cadavers: fare subject to negotiation."

"SANGLA" means "GOLD".

European tourists may also be intrigued to discover two competing shops selling hopia (a Chinese pastry) called Holland Hopia and Poland Hopia, which are owned and operated by two local Chinese entrepreneurs, Mr. Ho and Mr. Po, respectively.

"BAWAL UMIHI DITO PAG WALANG NAKATINGIN" means "IT IS FORBIDDEN TO PEE HERE WHILE NOONE'S LOOKING."

According to Manila businessman Tonyboy Ongsiako there is so much wit in the Philippines because

GOVERNMENT WARNING!

PLS. DON'T THROW YOUR
CIGARETTES END
ON THE FLOOR.
THE **COCKROACHES**
ARE GETTING **CANCER.**

". . .we are a country where a good sense of humor is needed to survive. We have a 24-hour comedy show here called the government, and a huge reserve of comedians made up mostly of politicians and retiring actors."

Projection 2   **Funny Love**

Tonyboy: (clears throat)

Your laugh is an infection
You are a blessing in the sky
You cut to the cheese
You bake your cake & lie in it
    in the wink of an eye

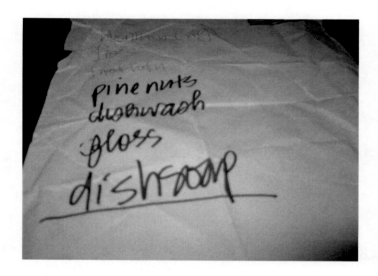

It was a no-win-win situation
It was as brand as new
It was clean as a daylight
    for me

"Hi, I'm Tonyboy," I said. "What's yours?"

I couldn't help myself to it
you rip what you saw
the sky's the langit, &
I am only human nature

Field Report

[Field Report. Page 1. Blank.]

Bigfoot Investigator: Follow-up investigation report. I was able to visit with the witness and his family, and explore the area over two days. The area has a rich wildlife environment - plenty of forest cover, creeks, berries, and orchards. There were also signs of deer in the area. The main encounter occurred in April, 2006, when he'd seen a creature staring at him through one of his windows. He noticed that he couldn't see his neighbors' light shining through the window, and noticed something blocking it out. At first he wasn't sure what he was seeing, but after staring at it for a number of seconds, he realized it was something that was looking back at him. At this point, he tried to push his door shut, which was open to let in a breeze. Something was holding it against his push, and he wasn't able to budge it, so he ran and woke his wife up and grabbed a firearm. He didn't hear anything after the incident, and nothing entered his house.

I inspected the window that the creature was looking through and was able to estimate that it stood about eight feet tall. The witness states that the creature's shoulders sloped into its head, almost as if it didn't have a neck, and the head was pointed at the top. The shoulders were extremely wide. The eyes were very dark, and yellowed and bloodshot around the edges. There was also a scar above the right eye that stood out.

The creature watching him in the window still scares the witness to this day. For a few months he was reluctant to be outside alone late at night. This is one of the few things he's ever been scared of in his life, and he says he'll never forget it.

The witness supplied this drawing:

Field Report. Page 2, drawing of Bigfoot.]

Projection 4　　　　　　**from LMFAO**

[from LMFAO. Full-screen, continuous slide projection beginning on page 22.]

set appro on single page
insert OBB & dialogue into

favorite comic panels
single word canvases

use language of comics to narrate OBB

(duh

single page jokes
give each statement its panel
& illustration.

eg. Im so taba!

(Cacay squeezing her
bilbil in front of
camera.)

or : static head shot of

Cacay or appr image with

balloons of statements

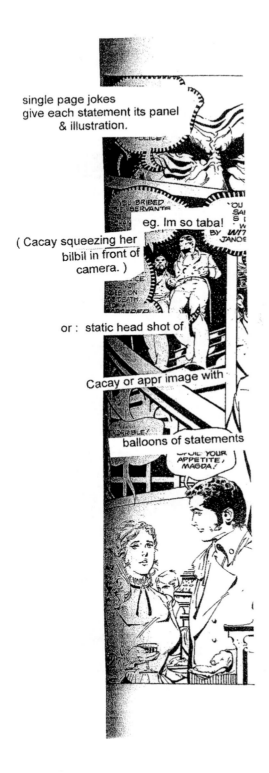

I never had a penny to my name —
so I changed my name.

You won't, I know, not for me.

That is, until I make more money.

42

I did.

He went and stole

my act .

(bad remembered

jokes.)

Filipino humor!!

"I like the biker chick
photos ."

"(Looks like Barbara Streisand.)"
"Looks like Rebecca Sherman!"

(LOL)

Why are all my close guy friends REPUBLICAN ??

They   collude in a   male   taking / of ownership,

LMFAO

modern - day biker   to   the   roaming frontiersman

47

how about doing a series of narrative inquiries into available

Bigfoot photographs? so you can make a chapbook of it

& hold a slide reading presen t a t i o n ? these are serious

investigations into the pheno m e n a but also open to train

of thought entering the writing my thickening accents of worship

unstinted belief scaffold brooding means indicative

treeline snaking limbed photography evidence constable

love in the after noon outdoor shack cusp day Albert

Ostman snaking the highway drunk with python fancy

I never said I conclude they exist but I do I do

believe in Bigfoot the possibility of—permanent imagination

not everything discovered yet to be uncovered cryptid

worship keep a journal of all your sites online belief is/as witness

writing is writing every thing turns in two . you say ocean pretend
lengthwise pretzel ouster weekend hopeful rest .

ie period, Prince started to hand-copy
he pages of the e images, and *Playboy*
se straightforwa ions were
l by a more laye uring the sam ive form of
which silk-scre rtoons from t graphics
agazines. The
on succeedec
propriation in

combine & recombine handwritten & printed jokes

song lyrics

news articles

advertising copy

with graphic snippets of appro cartoons .

reduce comic images to visual shorthand

transpose fragmented elements from their original settings

to the canvas

add silkscreen blur found photographs

51

People   keep   silkscreening   asking

found   photographs

appropriated cartoons

53

?

? ?

Larry Alcala

inquirer

an homage to
your child hood
love comics

Your laugh is an infection
You are a blessing in the sky
You cut to the cheese
You bake your cake & lie in it
in the wink of an eye

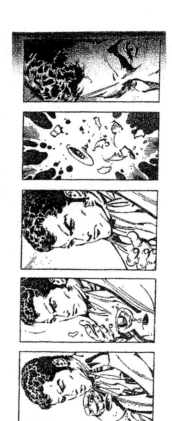

"Sometimes you look like you have Down Syndrome."

Which side are you on

the sound

cut out boxes of text from OBB

present these as sudden nights on

the page appro your

SELF

LMFAO

I dont know what to do

Ive been in love

I know this guy

each new body of work

is a cultural provocation

an invitation to think

of an already accepted
reality.

"Sometimes it feels like Im being had."

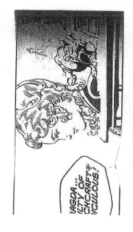

It was a no-win-win situation
It was as brand as new
It was clean as daylight
for me

"Hi, I'm Paolo," I said. "What's yours?"

I couldn't help myself to it
you reap what you saw
the sky's the langit, &
I am only human nature

If I dont Ill see you Wednesday

"How do we maintain, sustain ours..

look online for Max Blagg

concrete crosse S

Oh   Henry

Was that a girl   Was that a girl

Was that a girl

70

White Man: "I don't know what to do. My house has burned to the ground, my wife died

(staring at the sun)

Wolfgang Amadeus Bigfoot

Production Note

Generate static and/or moving images prompted by words appearing in caps throughout the dialogue. Once you've determined your selection, project it during the performance in the order of your choosing.

		[DULCET ENTER.
		PROJECTION]

ART BELL   First of all
                Ive got a MAP
                To the burial location
                Of two creatures
                We'll decide as
                The program wears on
                What these creatures are
                Im going to introduce
                Three people
                Robert W—
                Are you there?

ROBERT W   Listening
                With *both* ears

ART BELL   All
                Right
                Robert—
                Nobody's found you for a while

ROBERT W   Im living
                Somewhere
                In Montana
                And Im here
                On PURPOSE

ART BELL   So
                Your quest continues

ROBERT W   A
                Promise
                To get well

ART BELL   Did you write a book?

ROBERT W	No
	But I did an
	AUDIOCASSETTE
ART BELL	Well
	These days
	It comes—
ROBERT W	It comes
	It comes
	It comes
ROBERT W	
ART BELL	And goes!
ART BELL	I may have another
	Chapter for you here
	As the ah
	STORY
	Unfolds
ROBERT W	Folded
	Folded
	Folded
	Folded
ART BELL	With the time we've got
	Bugs—
BUGS	From the beginning?
ART BELL	Discuss
	Discuss
	Discuss
	This COURAGE

BUGS	I believe this
	Is December 76
	Or January 77
	A couple of buddies
	By the name of
	Bird Dog and Tim
	We're out hunting these
	VARMINTS
	COATS
	BOBCATS
	COONS
	Boy—
ART BELL	
ROBERT W	BOYYYY!
BUGS	A lotta nights
	We'd go out
	And hunt
	And come home with
	TWO THOUSAND DOLLARS
ART BELL	And by the way
	This is in TEXAS
BUGS	This is
	In Texas
ART BELL	PANHANDLE
	Of Texas
BUGS	That is correct

ART BELL   I guess we can identify *that* part
             Okay
             Go ahead

BUGS   And you know we travelled
             An hour with spotlight
             Going back and forth
             Looking for EYES

ART BELL   (The necessary
             Silhouette
             Uknown)

BUGS   Another hundred fifty yards
             Almost north of it
             And Bird Dog jumped out
             Come across the tab with his
             Ah
             RIFLE
             Ah and he says ah to me
             Something to the effect—

ART BELL   "What the heck is that?"

BUGS   Tim jumped out the pick-up
             Put his rifle on it
             And I put mine on it
             And I said—

ROBERT W   "I think it's a BEAR!"

BUGS   Cuz it was squatting out there
             In the middle of the wheat field
             And I said—

BUGS	
ART BELL	
ROBERT W	"LETS KILL IT!"

BUGS

We three fired at the same time
Ah it dropped we jacked
Another round into chamber
And it got up took off
And we fired again
And it dropped again
And it ran and jumped the fence
Down to the creek

ART BELL

FENCES…
In a row

ROBERT W

Who are they
Protecting
in ROME?

BUGS

It was running like a HUMAN
And we could see blood drops—

ART BELL

This
Is
Caes-
Sae-
Rea-
An
This
Is
Caes-
Ar—

ROBERT W	Dis- Dis- Dissident—
BUGS	And me being young And dumb And having a .44 MAGNUM Bird Dog he had a .357 And Tim he had a .22 So they said *You* got the big gun YOU GO IN
ART BELL	Like a RIOT
ROBERT W	Like a RHINO!
BUGS	I fired again Over backwards it went And hit the ground We looked at 'em, and Art It scares me to this day still That female Had BREASTS Just like a woman…
ART BELL	Watch Her Move In Elliptical Patterns

ROBERT W   SISTER—
                Do you remember when
                Twenty one years was old?

BUGS   And so me
                Bird Dog and
                Tim decided
                Best thing is to
                Bury them SUCKERS

ART BELL   It doesn't matter
                What you did…

ART BELL
ROBERT W   If you done it
                Like you been
                TORN

                                                    [SYNCOPATION.]

ART BELL   Did you think
                 You were looking
                 At a meat-eater
                 Or a vegetarian?

BUGS   If MICHAEL JORDAN
                 Wears size eighteen…

ROBERT W   You must be within
                 A hundred miles of
                 The Arkansas border

BUGS   …And *six* toes.
                 SIX TOES!

ROBERT W	I once tracked a family In Arkansas that did Have a six-toed GENETIC CODE
BUGS	We felt we had done shot some—
BUGS ART BELL ROBERT W	MENTALLY RETARDED PEOPLE
ART BELL	Follow. Misguide. Stand still.
BUGS	And the male The MALE organ—
ART BELL ROBERT W	(Hee Hee)
ART BELL	This love's For GENTLEMEN only!
ROBERT W	WEALTHIEST Gentlemen only!
BUGS	And it's still burned Into my brain To this day

[SYNCOPATION.]

ART BELL   All right
           That was then
           This is now
           Wild Card line—
           In Alberta, Canada
           Todd S—
           A conservationist
           Of these creatures—
           Here is an opportunity
           You won't want to pass up

TODD S   Disgust
           Disgust
           Disgust
           DISCOURAGE

BUGS   Todd
           Remember—
           We were out hunting
           For a LIVING

TODD S   I stand
           Outside
           Under
           Broken leaves

ART BELL   Let burn
           The cigarette
           Somewhere…

TODD S   Down
           And
           Lit
           From the bottom
           There's a misfit

ART BELL	True And Everlasting Didn't last *that* long
ROBERT W BUGS	HE- HE- HEY!

[SYNCOPATION.]

ART BELL	A lot of people think Bigfoot Is some sort of PARANORMAL Creature
BUGS	No This was An ANIMAL
ART BELL	Any of you seen Or know of Behavior Like it?
ROBERT W	Once I went to those Identical Areas And they left me GIFTS…
ART BELL	Theyre TELEPATHIC

ROBERT W	Theyre EMPATHIC
TODD S	Lonesome Lonesome Yeah
ART BELL	Bugs— You did not know it was a bigfoot You did not fire on it as a bigfoot
TODD S	Ask FORGIVENESS You know somewhere You're fixed to an atom
ROBERT W	But think of The furtherance For science
TODD S	They're in eminent danger
ROBERT W	They're in NEVADA
TODD S	They're in OKLAHOMA
ROBERT W	They're in CAROLINA
TODD S	They're in WEST VIRGINIA
ROBERT W	They're in ALABAMA
TODD S	They're in FLORIDA
ROBERT W	They have their own Routes

TODD S	They never have to Worry about the WEATHER—
ROBERT W	They have thrown ROCKS So close they missed My wife's head…
ART BELL	Well That's Fairly PRIMITIVE Right up there With CLUBBING
ROBERT W	I don't know about that, Art PALESTINIANS Are getting shot For throwing rocks
ART BELL	Well They claim With RUBBER BULLETS
TODD S	THE GOVERNMENT Is scared
ART BELL	Do you think—?
ROBERT W	I KNOW It's the case
TODD S	THE GOVERNMENT Has SATELLITES

Over that area
Right now

ROBERT W THE GOVERNMENT
Knows where
Those bones are
Right now

TODD S Tomorrow morning
Those bones
Won't be there

ROBERT W I would be damned
Disappointed
If THE GOVERNMENT
Didn't monitor your show

ART BELL Oh
THEY
Do

BUGS Im telling them:
"Show us
HIS
Birth certificate!"

ART BELL
ROBERT W
TODD S Time to show up
Time to show up
Time to show up!

ART BELL Shouldn't these
Creatures have

The same
    CIVIL RIGHTS
Under law?

TODD S
ROBERT W   Ab
                So
                    Lute
                        Ly.

ROBERT W   Did you know a
            Retarded
            Person
            Can VOTE?

                                                        [SYNCOPATION.]

BUGS   Art, you are the one person
            Who brings forth the stuff
            Everybody else laughs at

TODD S   "My people
            Are destroyed
            From a lack of
            KNOWLEDGE…"

BUGS   And someday
            You will get the last laugh
            Because you'll have
            THE PROOF

ART BELL
ROBERT W
TODD S   Fold it
            Fold it
            Fold it
            Fold it

BUGS	But the problem is Everybody in this Part of the world Knows who *I* am
ART BELL	Thank you, Bugs
BUGS	Good night, Art
ART BELL	Farewe- We- We- We- We- We- Well—
ROBERT W TODD S	I've been Looking for SOMETHING ELSE!
BUGS	Good night, Robert
ROBERT W	Farewe- We- We- We- We- We- Well—
TODD S ART BELL	No I gotta be SOMEONE ELSE!

89

BUGS   Good night, Todd

TODD S   Farewe-
              We-
              We-
              We-
              We-
              We-
              Well—

ROBERT W
ART BELL   Do
                You
                  Know
                     Me
                       Well?

ART BELL   GURLFRIEND…

ART BELL
ROBERT W
BUGS
TODD   HEY GURL HEYYY!   [PROJECTION REST
                                       DULCET EXIT.]

90

Heart as Arena

Batman That One

the   Joker is here/A.D./Bat symbol swoop into death building/a bank window a
building window explodes/market collapse insane plunge rooftop to rooftop/BANG!/
Camera i n place with music action/research how you enter safe

why does manager have a shotgun in/his office/vigilanteeism/Gotham in disrepair/
Where did you/this is a mob bank

what doesnt kill you simply makes you/ stronger/**Q U E E R**/bigfoot

Who Shot Ya/an artist a martial artist/will the real DK show up/LOITER/INTIMIDATE

dont point that thing at me/ hes bleeding/I   dont   need   help/ the difference/duality/hockey
pants/under that make-up/lipstick /on a/pig

oh so fly under the rubble/know your limits/its my fathers only wish/Batman fathered all of
them/Male in China??/buy American/fuck this D.A./lynching irradiated bills/Kaiser SMITH/i n
China   in China

you   want to be able to form your bad/hello   Mike   Keaton/someone like you
one final vinegar with my pals…../cut to/criminals gathering/the bad guys are
non - WHITE/or/-WASP

a guy like me/**FREAK/ CHINAMAN** is a squealer/lets not blow this out of proportion / the camera circle/the good guys/slippery point of view

Batman Hong Kong/Helen referred to Batman shrine/and then/made his own/ how about writing your own/MACROSS movie/did research of CIA use conspiracy threads

Batman has limits/Why so serious/**Father/Fathers/BATMAN** is insane **CHINAMAN**/is an object

Italian/Eastern European/leader of crime syndicate/ will/the real BATMAN/please stand/ up?/**Joker Joker /**I m a man of my word/Sun as Wayne suggests Death/ it all goes to/hell/from here/I dentity/I dentity/I dentity/J o ker/WHITE FACE/an undertone of /critique of white society/ THUG/All dark culture

BATMAN/consume blackness/to fight/the Darkness/blackness/Dark Knight/Joker disrupts an All White Party/all the money makers in Gotham/ **WHITE/** I hated my father

Watch the world burn/two sides of the same coin/WHITE MAN caped crusader/WHITE MAN serial killer/The rat is a LATINA cop/A critique of the White Man/The Dark Knight/is/the White Man

Batman can make the choice/Iam the Batman/I am the Batman/I am the Batman/Like the Mothman,   a harbinger/Fortean/You make

your own luck/**LYRIC OPERA**/Slaughter is the/Best Medicine/the workers/on break/get to see/a rich man's/toy emerge from/a car that they/historically may/have built

What would I do/what/ you/You complete me/to them/youre just a freak/like me/Its a bad joke/Only as good as the   world allows them/to be

Joker   doesnt   bleed/That guy was in Seinfeld/He sees his reflection/in the/gasoline/the Chinaman is a coward/Why should I hide/Who I am

Wheres the Italian? / THE TRUE IDENTITY OF BATMAN REVEALED/THIS town/tell your men/they wont work for a freakEverything burns/Ive had a change of heart/Let s give someone a chance

the nurse/the night nurse/your men your plan/Im a dog chasing cars/ I just do things/I try to show the schemers/how pathetic/ their attempts to control schemes/are/Nobody panics/when a gangbanger is shot

It s all part of/the plan/Lipstick on a/ Im an agent of chaos/Not Anarchy NIHILISM/FEAR/EMERGENCY/Death/Joker in drag/AMB ULANCE

Joker is a white man in whiteface/we cannot MISIDENTIFY/ his race/
BOMB BLAST LEVELS/DOUBT Fires/BATMAN sign in next scene
"Beautiful ."/This istoo much power/sonartapping
I want whomever let go/of the/let him off/the leash/you get to know

the real person/moments before they die/**IDENTITY OF GOTHAM S**

PUBLIC/criminal & civilian/Harvey has his limits/murdering white
civilians/decide on who s criminal/in **THEIR** society

SONAR POV/Perception in the/**d**ark/the big bad black
prisoner/stares down the white officer/ w/ mutton/
and offers to
person better/and here we go/and/here/we/go

It all boils down to/decision of/white men/we are still/Goths/at their
mercy/whiteface staring down midnight/youre alone/I cant rely on

anyone
these days upside down/
camera/moves upside down/
unstoppable fiend

meets/immovable object/truly/incorruptible/ I think I/Till their spirit

breaks completely/ I took Gotham s/
White Knight/and brought him/ down

to our/ l e v e l /

madness / like / gravity / a little push
the winner is / Gordon s blonde / blue eyed / son / someone

whom Harvey Dent / once was / there is no escape from
this / what s fair

the world is cruel / only morality / is chance / combined
unprejudiced / fair / because you were the best of us /
like I lied / **Lie** / it s going to be alright, son

see yourself / become / the villain / I killed these
people / Batman / Batman / because we have to chase him

the hero Gotham deserves / but doesn t need / right now

96

gh_t

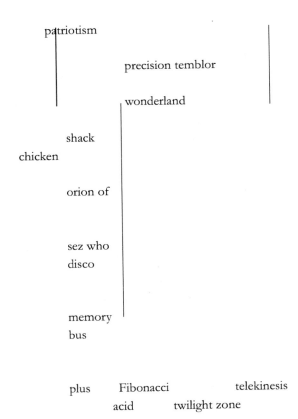

patriotism

precision temblor

wonderland

shack
chicken

orion of

sez who
disco

memory
bus

plus   Fibonacci   telekinesis
         acid   twilight zone

                              box
                 tear
                 Thick
                 the micas
                     censory
cup gave

                     yeah
                 drowning
                              you must

                     spank

                              ha
                 socialization

                              out deo
                         opprobrium

                         bought
                 orifice   tabula

98

fuzzy song logic

her

unity

algorithm

jarring

penis

te

nderness

from   hey R2D2

optic geek_{tomorrow}

goosing the

hypocrite

arrivederci_{China Moon}

off-the-rack supine

macho

Sith

blue

find away

jazzy

sugar dark

placebo

Lion heart

torture

build bingo

history

to keep _{insect}

theology   buck

zigzag

Papa Doc   bass

out of

Dionysus   flee

saw   trigger my god

eucalyptus

baby talk

paw

      shove spread-

eagled   party defect

    child why now

        gush

           of

      shocked

lips

          till

   the word

sound of light   reflex

    poster

gh

  undoing   like   self-flux

     cut

nationalism

                    cutesy dupest   wishes
                       vituperative
                                          jamboree
                                 shoe-polish dead yet
              are we
       flirtation

            independent
                  pinky shadows
Batcave
    shoat

                    edamam
                    e

                    as a

                    come-on

after sex

rub my

heartland

tsunami sashimi   mouth shove   gag
                                              copic

sprawled
surrender

ahoy

                        G
oldilocks

| | |

atom

syllogism   fake

hello   spastic

back

micros
DNA

Heart as Arena

Stupid white boys
Stupid white boys

'Ok you deserved that!'

stupid white boy
dumb motherfucker
want your face
    smeared across
      one of his
        paintings?

walk right up to me
stand right next to me
stupid dumb white motherfucker
   baggy   jeans   my   ass

cross your arms
my shit

the skull!!

a decent descent

skull & crossbones

oy   Jean-Michel
          tangina, pre

who's laughing now
          raging
     all the way to the
               corner bodega

in the clouds where
former champs gather

oy bodega

before belts beliefs were in fashion

im sorry I didn't brace up
to receive you in writing
but I awoke groggy this morning
one of six philistines missing

I'd love to break the jawbones
            of an ass
& serve it to him on a plate
stupid dumb dog motherfucker

      - -----

    (blank black)

clarification: I don't hate white people
I only resent
most
straight white
men, typically, until
proven human.

(an old white couple)

OWW: *'Why are the words all*
　　　upside down?'
OWM: *'Maybe his world was*
　　　at this point.'
OWW: *'No, it's only '82.'*

Santo
Versus
Second
Avenue

upside down
written
Chinese menu

two dollar
two dollar

mimics
a bleeding man
spiky red lines of hair

black tar and feathers

'I like this one, Ma.
It looks happy.'

PAW
PAW

"Eye and Eggs"

when two white people
gaze at you, darkie
white eye   black pupil
& a foggy pair of
they will only point out
      either

            the tracks of
            your kicks across
                  the canvas

                  or

                        which brush

tho I am not the
undiscovered genius
of the Mississipi
Delta I do know
who Mark Twain is
& all he's done to
shed light on
o ur terrible costs

all of us

Negroes
Negroes
Negroes

die   pork
it   product
rich

his closed
universe
of marks

an idea
distilling
into
meanderings
of
line

C P R K R

Luis, you never
   come to any
      of my readings

built by men of China
for chump change in 1850

why won't white folks
ever call it what
it is?

    a missed sipping
    a musty reeve

       a few small remains
drivel nails into
     your coughing

    two daytime Tylenol capsules
two nighttime Tylenol capsules

PERISHABLE

HEART AS ARENA
PROMETHEUS PASSPORT
Flashbulb
Drablo
Gina (ditto)

fuego

flores

Monty & Turtle

00:00:00	How do you frame a memory?
00:00:07	It's a question that burns throughout Wong Kar-Wai's cinema.
00:00:08	And of his nine feature films—
00:00:10	all

astonishing

in their beauty and formal daring—there's none
I can better remember

than *Happy Together*.

For one, I love how the film's synaptic rhythms enact
the discarded feelings of its characters.

How its style and love story weren't intellectualized into being,

00:00:28	or even planned.

How both were less about 'choice' or 'concept', and more about
'organic' or 'not imposed.'

You follow your instincts for what's possible in this space and what
two people in this situation are most likely to do.

00:00:38	MONTY:	*This is your coat?*
		Sorry.
	TURTLE:	*Excuse me.*
	MONTY:	*No prob.*
		Sorry I fell asleep on it.
		Im Monty by the way.
		Terrible!
00:01:01		*Sometimes I forget my own name.*
	TURTLE:	*That's o-kay.*
		I forget mine all the time too.
	MONTY:	*Well it's nice to…*
	TURTLE:	*…meet you.*

PAUSE

00:01:10	When people ask how did we meet, I tell

the truth: Kim's party at Tangerine,
seconds after I decide to leave it,
descending fog of malicious ex is
swept away by the sudden gale of your

00:01:25	laugh

00:01:30	When he began *Happy Together*, Wong Kar-Wai only had two characters in mind: Tony and Leslie's.
00:01:36	He'd managed to find a city to put them in, but nothing else.
	What did they feel when they came to Argentina?
	Did they know it would be so cold in the summer?
00:01:46	In improvisatory filmmaking, solutions always present themselves at the very last minute.
	Maybe they aren't even real solutions, but something always turns up to solve the problem.
00:01:55	The idea is to tell the story of these two people, but because of time limits Wong knows he can't make a film about two people.
00:02:03 FADE OUT	
00:02:05 FADE IN	

	MONTY:	*So watcha doin?*
	TURTLE:	*It's a one-winged bird.*
00:02:12		*It's kind of flying this way.*
		I guess it's a mallard.
00:02:15	MONTY:	*How can you tell its head?*
00:02:23	TURTLE:	*It has a beret right here because it's a surrealist.*
	MONTY:	*You mean fascist looking angelic to recover face.*
	TURTLE:	*Ha-ha.*
		Everything is a little bit mumble.

00:02:37 DISSOLVE	On our first date, you suggested *Lilya-4-Ever*, a film about an Estonian teenager who is abandoned by her mother, forced into white slavery, then commits suicide.
CLOSE ON	What were you thinking?
00:02:52	Despite the film, it was such a gas after to walk up University Place with you, especially when you offered me a bag of
	dried mangoes
	to eat.
	"Why, because I'm *Filipino*?" I teased.

124

You were so embarrassed.

Thankfully, our second film, which we both knew was a comedy
in advance, made up for the first one:

a *Mighty Wind* by Christopher Guest.

00:03:10   I remember how you and I kept rolling in our seats because of the
recurrence of the Cabana Boy character—a Filipino extra whose
sole function was to smile broadly for the camera in each scene.

Watching him play with gusto such a transparently token
person of color in the movie was absurd to the point of hilarity.

The five or so other people in the theater kept motioning to shut
up, but it was too late: giddiness had taken over,
would bind us forever

00:03:30
to that moment's character.

00:03:40   Both of these films ended up being the only ones we'd catch until
the fall, when we decided to give it another shot.

The next would be *Lost in Translation* by Sophia Coppola, a movie
whose cinematography draws heavily from the style of
Christopher Doyle, Wong Kar-Wai's go-to DOP.

00:03:52
And, much like Wong's film, Coppola's luxuriates in the themes of
dislocation and closeness versus the impossibility

00:04:02
of love,

in dynamism versus the need to hold on.

00:04:15

00:04:21

00:04:22   TURTLE.   *"Allow me to*
                      re-intro
00:04:27 FADE OUT   *duce myself*
                      my name is HOV
00:04:28 FADE IN   *H to the OV*
                      I used to move snowflakes
00:04:32   *by the O-Z!"*

Robert Rauschenberg said you're not an artist if you can't walk a
block and come up with five new images, and even more ideas.

Edward Steichen said you can photograph a world in your room, and later Robert Frank and Keiichi Tahara showed us how to.

00:04:44	Chris Doyle finds a stairway, an entrance, a wall he likes. He starts to get a feel for the kind of characters who would use such a space. So he has fun turning the camera on and off at will, to generate the
00:05:00	effect of random spontaneity, like a series of
00:05:15 CLOSE ON	polaroid snaps

that skip through time and disregard any continuity.

00:05:22	*MONTY:*	*You know, I could use a ride up to my residency next month.*
00:05:24		*It's up in the Valley.*
	TURTLE:	*Pretty!*
	MONTY:	*What do you say?*
	TURTLE:	*Mos def.*

00:05:35 DISSOLVE

00:05:37 *Happy Together* and its characters are all out of time and out of space. And Tony and Leslie struggle to repair their relationship in the most difficult reality:

00:05:45 as gay Chinese nationals in a xenophobic country neither one can fluently speak the language.

00:05:54	*TURTLE:*	*Um, this is my friend Monty.*
	MONTY:	*Monty.*
		Hi.
	TURTLE:	*This is Jamie.*
		Wow, you look mumble.
	JAMIE:	*Are you still making images?*
	TURTLE:	*Mumble mumble yes no.*
		My finger doesn't mumble press like this.
	JAMIE:	*Oh, too bad.*
	TURTLE:	*Are you mumble culinary school?*
	JAMIE:	*Yes, still, you know, cooking away.*
	TURTLE:	*Wow, that's fantastic.*
		Mumble mumble mumble…?

00:06:26 (Tony and Leslie's interiors are consciously timeless, not logically lit.)

00:06:29 FADE OUT
            PAUSE

00:06:30 FADE IN

00:06:31	Tony keeps a souvenir lampshade of Iguazu Falls.
	The light passing through the holes in the cylinder make the water painted on the plastic shade part
00:06:41	seem to cascade downward.
00:06:42 FADE OUT	
00:06:43 FADE IN	Chris Doyle once claimed his best films were made when he was saddest and just out of love.
	He was very much in love when he began *Happy Together*, so he assumed his then relationship with Denise wouldn't end so good.
00:07:00	She tells him: "It hurts, but I have to leave you."
00:07:22	"At least I know now you'll make a better movie."
00:07:30	The clouds moving the shadows across the road in random patterns, the traffic, and what's happening on the roadside
00:07:38	all
	affect
00:07:40	the shot.
00:07:42	Mix a dash of experience
00:07:44 FADE OUT	with a lot of intuition,
00:07:46 FADE IN	and try to think ahead, Doyle insists.
00:07:58	"All I know," he says, "is how I see the space…"
00:08:01	"…and what I hope I can do with it."
00:08:04 FADE OUT	
00:08:05 FADE IN	
00:08:08	That summer in the Valley, I lived in my artist studio.
00:08:14	I focused on work, staying up late
00:08:18	and crashing on the floor.

129

00:08:20	I wanted to de-familiarize myself, move out of certain spaces, preconceptions of the world
00:08:28 CLOSE	I knew so well.
00:08:29 DISSOLVE	
00:08:30	Chris Doyle writes how he would always associate the 'blurred action' sequences in his other films with Wong Kar-Wai with the adrenaline 'rush' that fear or a violent act excites.
00:08:40	In *Happy Together*, it's more druggy, the speed changes marking 'decisive', 'epiphanal', or 'revelatory' moments.
00:08:46	The actor moves extremely slowly while all else goes on in 'real time'.
00:08:53	The idea is to suspend time, to emphasize and prolong the 'relevance' of what's going on.
00:08:56 SILENCE	

to

00:09:04 FADE OUT	
00:09:06 FADE IN	
00:09:07	About a month after the blackout, you and I get back together.
00:09:12	Eight years now and counting.
00:09:17	I think about the ending of Wong's film, shortly after Tony's character wakes up from a long sleep in Taipei,
	the city of your birth.
00:09:34	He decides to visit Chang at their stall in the Liaoning night market,
00:09:38	but discovers
	his friend's family instead.
00:09:44	In voice-over, Tony reveals:

"I finally understood how he could be happy
running around
 so free.

00:09:54

It's because he has a place
he can always

00:10:02 FADE OUT

return to."

Feeling Its Actual

why did i always
use the wrong words
should be other words
that are more suitable
language is quite strange
and make me so confused
i often cannot understand
what they say
i want to hide in a place
that makes me comfortable
this sofa feels like
the peafowls feathers
very comfortable
make me feel ecstatic

i can also listen to the
tone of the foreign language
knowing that only this kind
of language express such
unique images and life
in fact i just need to imagine
what i want or fancy what
will be happened
if i dont want something
to happen, i go away
i miss my home too
time can stop in anytime
for the weather is cold
all day long

all day long
i miss my home
for the weather is cold
i dont want to go to school
going to school feels like carding
but mother wont help me
time wont stop just for you
time can stop in anytime
it can stop at six o clock
i can be this way concedingly
sounds she makes me to make

poopoo padoo
poopoo padoo

watching the red darner
being chased at sunset
memories—thats what i forget
i remember happy things
if the happy things
are what i remember
is that means i am sad
when i forget?
its not that i dont remember
i love to remember happy things
besides that i dont know
i cant remember a lot of things
id like to remember more
id like to know

the contrast, color, and sound
are independent
i always cant be clear
about all these things
too many colors and shapes
if we face the mirror
would become the same person
its something about the light
but i dont know what hes saying
hes only got one eye
but i think he is winking at me
egg is an old lady
their children is her stick
and this blue lamp
thats my auntie

so i was a house princess
and especially my dad was a king
to me and my mom was a queen
but things that i know a lot about
are musty woman things
things that ive learn from mom
i was following her footsteps
and i am too determined
to make my way alone
i was not a great cook but
i have a great eyes for details

'Your pillow is outside itself.'

Wishing on the 1

warm potato leek soup
warm buttered bread

blood flow to knees again
no more nosebleeds

a new hoodie
a cuticle remover

toasty toe socks
7 ride forever

We buy a four-person chopper
ride flown by Daniela and trainer.

We fly over the Napali Coast, &
famous celebrity beach homes.

We fly inside Mount Wai'ale'ale
bursting with new waterfalls.

We fly through rainbows, &
into mist.

Hurt my left hand squeezing this
railing into life.

air japan flight number 64
is scheduled for monday
thursday and friday
china air flight number 51
always delays
i stay at home but can
show up in different places
for example, i want to
go to the shop on the corner
but suddenly i see
the skyscraper becomes home
buying french fries in fast food
restaurant but thinking of paris
i often have such
clear images in my head

gold cup is pain
one is matchsticks
three is oranges
thirteen is blanket
thirty one is twenty seven cops
shark equals bus stop
shrimp equals wooden stick
turnip equals school bus red
snapper equals bath tub
peacock feather equals sofa
should say "boxes on the road"
the shark in the station
should say "taste of the times"

if im like a piece of bok choy
then you are probably
a piece of broccoli
but i do think we are in
the same pot
do you know what i mean
we are quite together
thats what i feel
its just the communication thing

Tangerina

Not to beat a round bush
But your laugh was an infection
So I cut to the cheese

What would I lose to gain?
You get to that chicken when
It crosses the bridge

When time is of the elements
You take things first at a time
Lalo na kung the feeling is actual

Sharmina Lair

repeat after me: MIKEE KYACO
hit those strap with bow
I love you Axl this is 4 you
gigzz gigzz giz i wnt more

I gonna rock ur world ur round
ur head ur circle ur harm
ur balls ur merchandize
ur general ur dead

Im sleepy see you in my dreams
the yellow bell hawaiian look
Im sick and tired but the blossom
face keeps on shining

i was always taking clothes apart
and putting them back together
in unusual ways
i couldnt talk to my dad for years
because of the choices i made
always away from home
pushing for some other things
he didnt think i should want
when ive already took
the wrong way
i walk toward the sea
the meaningless language
the noises and smells of the city
maybe he can see now that
i am strong and with good people

what
WU AY NI
need

paolo tian tian tan lian'ai

paolo lao gong
tian tian lao po

pingdeng
hunyin

xinhun kuaile
baitou xielao

bainian haohe javier liu

the sea is warm
and the horizon is soft
like the phrase "ebb and flow"
it likes to run toward the sea
windward at sunset
images those sounds
smell and places
shanghai? ive been there before
it feels like being embraced
by the deep blue sea
i dont want to leave here

給劉恬恬

Acknowledgments

Christopher Doyle, Bill Murray, Alex Niño, Nury Vittachi, Phoenix, Carl Wessler, Art Bell.

Ladies and Gentlemen—Mr. Bill Murray! was commissioned by the Asian American Writers Workshop for its Intimacy and Geography Poetry Conference, and performed on closing night with live electronic and film improvisations by Guillermo E. Brown and Vinay Chowdhry.

FYEO has been performed as a solo work at the Lower Manhattan Cultural Council in New York, and at Small Press Traffic's Poets Theater Festival in San Francisco (featuring Oakland poet Dennis Somera).

Wolfgang Amadeus Bigfoot was first presented at Semiospectacle: A Literary Revue, curated by Mashinka Firunts, at Performance Space 122 in New York City, with the following cast: 劉恬恬 (ART BELL), Thomas Fink (ROBERT W), and Geoffrey Olsen (TODD S). Digital projections by Mashinka and John Harkey.

Monty & Turtle was filmed at the *Be Kind Rewind* installation at Deitch Projects. Shot and co-edited with Vicente Pouso, *Monty & Turtle* stars the following: Emmy Catedral (MONTY), Yuan Wu (TURTLE), Mary Ellen Obias (JAMIE), and 劉恬恬, Shivani Manghnani, and Marcus Borg (EXTRAS).

Cover photo by Emmy Catedral. Author photo by 劉恬恬. Illustrations for *Monty & Turtle* section and portrait of 劉恬恬 by Alex Tarampi (http://theimaginary.net). Book and cover design by Tim Peterson (Trace) (http://mappemunde.typepad.com).

Thank you, Marsh Hawk Press, Queens Council on the Arts, New York State Council on the Arts, Queens Borough President's Office, Dia Art Foundation, The Millay Colony, Poets House, Lower Manhattan Cultural Council, Queens Museum of Art, Queens Library, Space 37, Small Press Traffic, Asian American Writers Workshop, Poetry Project, Bowery Poetry Club, Unnameable Books, OMG!, creature press, *Aufgabe*, *The Capilano Review*, *MiPoesias*, *Shampoo Poetry*, *EOAGH*, 恬恬, Family, the Lius, Tom, Tim (Trace), Alex, Sandy, Rev. Nakamoto, N.S.T., Emmy, Mary Ellen, John, Del Ray, Brandon, Fred, Vincent, Kevin, Geoff, Despo, Lucille, Jill, Jonny, Courtni, Peter, Meredith, Remy, Peace Bros., Mai, Vicente, Shivani, Filip, Mark L., Mark R., Zack, Michelle, Parkmich, Ernest, Mike, Prerana, Vinay, Alan, Zehra, Jolyn, Carl, Lucy, Charles, Hutch, Electric Kulintang (Susie I. and Roberto), Stephen, Kate, Mashinka, Marcus, Nick, Susie T., Hector, Hong Yee, and Lynn.

About The Author

PAOLO JAVIER is the current Queens Borough Poet Laureate. He is the author of four chapbooks and two full-length collections of poetry, including *60 lv bo(e)mbs* (O Books) and *the time at the end of this writing* (Ahadada), which received a Small Press Traffic Book of the Year Award. The recipient of 2011 grants from the Queens Council on the Arts and New York State Council on the Arts, he's held writing residencies at the Lower Manhattan Cultural Council, The Millay Colony, and the AC Institute Dept of Micro-Poetics, and served as a Visiting Associate Professor in Poetry at the University of Miami. He edits and publishes 2nd Avenue Poetry, a tiny press devoted to innovative language art, and lives with his wife in Queens.

Other Books from Marsh Hawk Press

Peace Conference
Thomas Fink

Breaking the Fever
Mary Mackey

There's Only One God and You're Not It
Stephen Paul Miller

Under the Wanderer's Star
Sigman Byrd

What He Ought To Know
Edward Foster

Eminent Domain
Justin Petropoulos

The Good City
Sharon Olinka

If Not for the Courage
Daniel Morris

Whither Nonstopping
Harriet Zinnes

Inside the Ghost Factory
Norman Finkelstein

The After-Death History of My Mother
Sandy McIntosh

Almost Dorothy
Neil de la Flor

Somehow
Burt Kimmelman

At the End of the Day: Selected Poems and An Introductory Essay
Phillip Lopate

I Take Thee, English, for My Beloved
Eileen R. Tabios

Ernesta, in the Style of the Flamenco
Sandy McIntosh

After Taxes
Thomas Fink

Imperfect Fit
Martha King

The Thorn Rosary: Selected Prose Poems and New (1998-2010)
Eileen R. Tabios

Watermark
Jacquelyn Pope

Skinny Eighth Avenue
Stephen Paul Miller

Last Call at the Tin Palace
Paul Pines

Night Lights
Jane Augustine

Facing It: New and Selected Poems
Corrine Robins

Natural Defenses
Susan Terris

Bryce Passage
Daniel Morries

The Beginning of Sorrows
Edward Foster

One Thousand Years
Corinne Robins

Fort Dad
Stephen Paul Miller

Sharp Golden Thorn
Chard deNiord

Quantum Jitters
Patricia Carlin

House and Home
Rochelle Ratner

In Ways Impossible to Fold
Michael Rerick

Mirage
Basil King

Light Light or the Curvature of the Earth
Harriet Zinnes

Serious Pink
Sharon Dolin

Birds of Sorrow and Joy
Madeline Tiger

Ben Casey Days
Rochelle Ratner

Original Green
Patricia Carlin

A Woman's Guide to Mountain Climbing
Jane Augustine

The Bee Flies in May
Stephen Paul Miller

Mahrem: Things Men Should Do for Men
Edward Foster

Clarity and Other Poems
Thomas Fink

Either She Was
Karin Randolph

Reproductions of the Empty Flagpole
Eileen Tabios

Passing Over
Norman Finkelstein

Forty-Nine Guaranteed Ways to Escape Death
Sandy McIntosh

The Pond at Cape May Point
Burt Kimmelman and Fred Caruso

The Light Sang As It Left Your Eyes
Eileen Tabios

Arbor Vitae
Jane Augustine

Drawing on the Wall
Harriet Zinnes

The Elephant House
Claudia Carlson

Gossip
Thomas Fink

Blind Date with Cavafy
Steve Fellner

Between Earth and Sky
Sandy McIntosh

77 Beasts: Basil King's Bestiary
Basil King

For more information, please go to: http://www.marshhawkpress.org.